JASIRI BASEL

101
THINGS
I WISH MY
FATHER
TAUGHT
ME

BE

BE YOU
BE BRAVE
BE SMART
BE A LEADER
BE ENERGETIC
BE COURTEOUS
BE COURAGEOUS
BE HAPPY. BE WISE
BE BOLD. BE HONEST

Table of Contents

101
THINGS

Introduction

Why was this book written?

I'm under the belief that there are many males growing up without their fathers and without positive role models. In some instances, when the father is around, not all information is transferred to the son. Often, the father did not gain the information in his lifetime. Consequently there are gaps and holes that challenge the son from becoming a "whole man." This problem touches all races to some degree but in the black community it is an enormous problem that creates other problems that plague us in many ways. This book also puts focus on some of the 'elephants in the room' that the world often refuses to recognize as part of the problem.

Changing The Paradigm

As a young black male that grew up in a single parent house hold without my father and very few positive role models in my life, I know first hand of its impact and challenges. Even though at times I had those who wanted to help, I faced great challenges(alone) because many of them had never traveled the path I was on. This book seeks to provide, in advance, a range of insights to help shape a way of thinking and mold boys into men. It also seeks to help the men working to improve themselves. It is by no means an exhaustive account, but merely a starting point with some "tips" that have tangible value in real life.

1

"Learning is critical to life, and there is way more to be learned than what they teach in schools."

I t is knowledge that is important, not the educational system it self. There are plenty of ways to get knowledge and the traditional educational system in America is NOT the only way. From You-tube, to books, to travel, mentors, and seeing for yourself; knowledge is yours to have. Hands-on experience is certainly the only way to achieve mastery of subject. We must also keep in mind that often agendas are at work and what you will be taught by a structured system will be only what they want you to believe and will often exclude many truths that you need to know.

   Most structured systems are designed to create workers, employees, tax payers, and sheep. You must go beyond that and learn as many ways as you can. He who gets knowledge has an opportunity to get power.

2

The responsibility of the world is not yours to bear.

B eing an alpha male and having eyes open to the things that are going on in the world it is easy to feel the burden and the need to "fix it". What man doesn't want to right the wrongs of the world? Who doesn't want to fix the problems that burden us as a people? And who was born to do it? It all makes sense, but it isn't a reality... while we can do much to have impact, we can only do what we can do, to have that impact. In addition, if we attempt too much we risk 1) spreading ourselves too thin to be effective 2) Burning ourselves out and becoming no good to anyone(including ourselves).

Learning this took me many years. In fact , I still struggle with trying to save everyone while still risking myself. Have impact but do not succumb to the pressures you created.

3

The weight of the world is on your shoulders.

While it is true that the responsibility of the world is not yours to bear, as the man of the family, as a visionary and a leader there are plenty of things that will directly be placed on you to get done or you will feel compelled or responsible for them.

   Had I known early in life that my personal actions and decisions would have great impact to me, my family, my people and the future of the world, there is much I would have done differently. Though I might have learned it earlier than some I learned it much later than I wish I had. Be intentional in your efforts to positively impact the world and those around you.

4

Learn how to fight.

Over the years by "trial and error", studying, practicing and taking my licks I've become somewhat of a warrior (for someone with no military or formal training). Growing up I had too many fights to recall all of them. What's funny is that after a while of fighting and winning, you rarely have to fight any more(this in itself was a valuable lesson).

I have a few memories and situations I remember about my dad, and while he never taught me to fight I can recall a situation where he didn't let me run from a fight but made me stand up and fight back . At this time I had to be in early elementary school and I was outside playing and got jumped by 2 boys a little older than me and I ran inside. What I recall is that he made me go back outside and fight. While not something I wanted to do then, it was a valuable lesson as since then I've never

4

Learn how to fight.

been one to back down from a fight out of fear. I'm not saying I've taken ever opportunity to fight because frankly I think that is foolish. I however will 'fight' if something of great value is at stake and that's the ONLY way "out of the situation."

Foremost, learning to fight helps to develop a needed mentality for what we are up against in the world. Things won't come easy, what you believe is yours, others believe is theirs'; what you know is yours, some will try to take it from you if you let them. You have to be willing to fight(literally and figuratively), and after a while of gaining a reputation of fighting and winning, or fighting and putting a hurting on your opponent, people are less likely to pick fights with you. In addition sometimes you simply have to fight for those who can't fight for themselves. Remember to leave physical fights as a last resort; instead use your brain as the primary tool in which you do battle.

5

Decide what's worth fighting for.

Everything simply isn't worth fighting for, even if you are sure to win. Often times it's a waste of energy, resources and the consequences aren't always what's intended. Just because you can fight, and even if you are "guaranteed" to win, sometimes the wisest choice isn't to fight.

Knowing in advance what is worth fighting for will help you make better decisions and take positive actions.

6

Learn how to pick your battles.

O nce you know how to fight and what's worth fighting for, picking your battles is where the wisdom comes in.

Being powerful is wonderful, but being strategic is key to winning. If you are playing to win, its critical to be prepared to fight, and to fight for what's worth it, but you also don't want to be in constant battles. You don't want to wear yourself down and you don't want to be injured and or defeated in a battle that won't have a measurable impact on the overall war. Choose wisely, but don't use being careful and strategic as an excuse to be a coward.

7

You will face adversity and challenges simply for being a black male.

✈B

In short, the world (especially America), has a deep "hatred" for blacks and black men. Although I didn't quite understand why, this is something I learned early in life. Initially I thought things would change with education, then with money, then with status and so on and so forth; but the reality is: "By and large simply being black over rides almost all other things and makes accomplishing many things more challenging."

Do not use this as an excuse for not achieving, not taking action or for not having impact; in fact...use it as fuel to help your excellence. Despite this challenge you can overcome and achieve great things. You can impact the world and others. Even if given the opportunity I wouldn't choose to be anything other than a black male.

8

Learn to build and do carpentry.

I have come to believe that there are a certain skill sets that all men should possess. As men we should be able to build structures, to make improvements and to create. I first took notice to carpentry when I visited my best friend's home(the nicest house I had been in at the time). I was impressed with the home, but more impressed to discover that his dad built it (down to the smallest details) himself. Now, years later, I have the skills to just about build a house from the ground up. A man who can build has the power to provide housing for his family in event of some major catastrophe or simply fix things when they go wrong. Building is sometimes about simply being able to get an idea out of your head and into reality. To take raw materials and create something is power! Building and carpentry also is a means of generating income without the need for a system. Harness and use your power!

9

Learn to cook.

If you want to eat you should know how to cook. Simple. (Point blank, no exceptions,no excuses). If you like food, then you should learn to master the art of cooking. I learned to cook initially out of "survival", then I grew to like it, and eventually I began on the road to mastery. It's a never ending road as I continue to try different ingredients, seeing different dishes from different countries and cultures, I'm constantly blending, mixing and creating unique things with my own touch.

Though my father never taught me to cook, one of the few things I remember about our interactions was him cooking awesome baked chicken after picking me up from school a couple of times. All who knew him well, said he was an awesome cook. So in some way I guess it was handed down.

10

Learn to grow food.

F ood is essential to life, food is essential to cooking. Healthy food is essential to fighting and keeping disease away. The world and our culture has largely gone away from growing their own food. The majority of what we consume is corporate controlled, tainted and not good for our bodies. Most people have no idea about the obvious connection between food, health and disease. Being able to grow your own food gives you better control over your own life(not to mention, agriculture is big business). **"Let food be thy medicine and medicine be thy food." - Hippocrates**

I love to cook with different fresh and raw seasonings. I use food for healing and prevention; making this a part of my lifestyle has produced excellent results.

11

Begin with the end in mind.

Everything in life begins somewhere and ends somewhere. Too often as we begin things, we do not think about the end result we wish to achieve or the consequences of our initial actions. It is important for you to have a vision for your life, what you want to accomplish and purpose behind the activities you participate in. This vision will help you plan and guide your steps to achievement. I'm not saying that your vision or end-goal won't change, or that it will be perfect. I am saying that knowing where you wish to end up, is a gigantic part of you getting there. If you have no where in particular you wish to go, any path will get you there. If you are reading this, you however wish to lead a life of significance and impact so, anywhere and anything simply isn't good enough. Think ahead, plan well, take action.

12

Learn to handle a firearm.

I came to understand that many middle class black families are seriously "anti gun", thus most have never handled a gun and don't want one in their houses.

Be it hunting or self-defense, knowing how to properly and responsibly handle a firearm is a skill I believe men should possess(even if rarely used). Do not wait until you need a skill to begin learning it. At that point it's a possibility it may be too late. **"It's better to be a warrior in a garden, than a gardener in a war."**

13

Learn to weld.

It goes back to building, creating and exercising power. Having a creative mind, I personally believe that welding is a skill that gives you the ability to build and equip many necessary elements of life. Welding is also a valuable skill that one can use to make a living.

Welding can be an asset in the "Create, Build & Grow" paradigm and also is one of those skills sets that will always allow you to keep your "freedom" by being able to run a business providing direct services to others.

14

Athletics aren't the only way to succeed.

By and large young black males are sold this picture that the only or best way for them to make it and succeed is to play sports and be an all star athlete . This is simply a fantasy and it sets many up for failure. The metrics alone make going pro for most impossible.

However, all can succeed by using their brains instead of just merely their physical abilities. There are plenty of fields that one can make a great living and even become a millionaire. Starting and building your own business will allow you to have unlimited earning potential. Build something you have control over, something you can leave behind and pass down. Don't be fooled into thinking that athletics is your only way.

15

Africa is nothing to be ashamed of.

From as far back as I can remember, just about all things that America told and ingrained into us regarding Africa was negative. Those who were darker were teased for being such as kid. We as a people didn't want to be associated with Africa because of what we thought we knew about the continent, its culture, and its people. Yet the reality is: Africa is absolutely nothing to be ashamed of, we should be proud. Africa is the beginning of man. Africa is the richest continent on the planet. Africa holds the greatest marvels known to man.

I learned later in life about the greatness of Africa, the greatness of our ancestors and the lies we are continually told to keep us from wanting to know more and explore the truth and history of our great continent. You should intentionally make it a priority to reconnect to the continent and its people. At all times, take pride in Africa!

16

Knowledge combined with the right action leads to power.

We are often told that "Knowledge is Power", this is somewhat of a lie or simply misleading. Knowledge alone is nothing but mere knowledge. It is the combination of knowledge mixed with the right action that gives us power.

If you want to be powerful, get knowledge and take the right action. To maximize your greatness you must compound everything you have ever learned in your actions and execution.

17

Keep it to yourself.

If you are planning something or working on something, it's important to keep it to yourself. Not everyone needs to know about your ideas and plans. Frankly only those who are assisting with, or a part of what you doing should be privy to such information. It is not until your execution is done that there is value in the general public knowing. It is then, that you should tell others.

Most people do not mean you or your ideas any good, so their knowledge of your ideas and plans is of no value. Get a grip on your excitement and desire to tell others and instead put that energy towards execution.

18

Do your best, EVERYDAY.

All that you can do, is what you can do. The key here is to ALWAYS do your best everyday in every situation. Doing so will increase your ability, your impact and will develop you as a person. In most areas of life there will be competition or at least perceived competition, and this is great because steel sharpens steel and competition is good for improvement. Keep in mind, you aren't really competing against them, you are competing against who you were yesterday. Your goal is to do your absolute best always and to be better today than you were yesterday.

19

Be a producer, not merely a consumer.

ᕙB

Every day we consume a countless amount of products and services. All of this consumption cost us something, and profits those who produce the products and services. This profit allows them to live the lives they desire and to provide for their families.

You are totally capable of being more than just a consumer. You have the ability to produce and profit! Set your mind to the reality that you can create a product or service that serves the needs of others. If you want to be in control of your life you must be in control of your finances. By becoming a producer, you can make that happen! In addition to being a producer be intentional about spending your dollars with businesses that are invested in you and the future of your community.

20

Love doesn't solve all problems.

There are many sayings about "love curing all" but the reality is that love does not solve all problems. From the interpersonal to the global problems that we all deal with; love alone is not enough to solve things. Interpersonally just because one loves a person doesn't mean the relationship can work out or that the love you have for someone will definitely morph them into something different.

Many times, love creates many of the problems we are left to solve. Love is critical but it is not always the answer. Be careful to not let your emotions and your "love" cloud your judgment and either directly or indirectly put you in a position to damage your life.

21

Not everyone who loves you will always tell you the truth.

An unfortunate reality of life is: You will be lied to by the people who love you. Some times its small, sometimes its huge. Sometimes they think they are helping by not telling the truth. Sometimes they don't know the truth, and have been given lies that they believe and those same lies are being passed down to you.

Just because they love you doesn't mean they are incapable of lying to you. Being aware of this gives you some degree of protection and at least a realistic perspective when/if it occurs. It's not their responsibility to give you the truth, but it is yours to find it. Trust but verify.

22

The truth won't always align with what you believe.

Merely believing something does not make it true. Many people believe many things that simply aren't truth; you are not excluded. Do not ever confuse your beliefs with the truth. Seek truth, demand and expect facts. Be logical and be sensible. Don't ever make a decision to not seek truth simply because you are afraid of having your beliefs dis-proven. Seeking truth will often mean you will walk alone, and you will be opposed and disliked for disrupting the untrue beliefs of others. Truth seekers are few in this age, be not afraid to learn whether your beliefs are true or false.

23

The truth won't always align with what your family or loved ones believe.

The same goes for your family, their beliefs won't always be truth either. This won't stop them from teaching those beliefs to you. We are deeply entrenched into culture that has been passed down; culture that most have never questioned or researched. Truth is more important and impactful than tradition. Whether we wish to admit it or not, often times people would rather hold on to their beliefs as opposed to knowing the truth. Do not be afraid to think for yourself, they will get over it. In fact, some of them may even learn from the knowledge you have gained or be inspired and motivated by your courage.

24

Control your anger and your emotions.

N o matter how strong you think you are, if you do not exercise control over your anger and emotions you will not be able to maximize your life and you are likely to be without power. Your emotions, when not mastered by you, will always put you under the control of someone else. "Emotional Intelligence" is a key to functioning in life on a level beyond most humans. This allows you greater communication, problem solving and ability to see further.

If you have any desire to lead and positively impact, you must posses the ability to stay in control of self.

25

Help others, but do not let doing so destroy you.

If you can... always help others, but keep in mind that often helping others takes something(mental, emotional, time, resources) from you. It is critical to know that even though you are helping people , that does not mean they care about you or have your best interest in mind . It is your responsibility to protect you and your life even while helping others.

If you have given so much that it hurts you, it makes it hard for you to continue to help others. Know that some people will take from you until you have no more, and move on leaving you without anything (including their help for you).

26

Protect, teach and love your family.

Family should be the most important element of life. Unity begins with your family. Look out for them, give them knowledge, give them love, build for their future. Work together and lead by example.

There will be times that the greatest challenges will come with them having to unlearn what they have been taught; be patient. There will be times that they will hurt you, be forgiving. Do not let disagreements about trivial things pull you apart; always make it a point to resolve conflict and move forward even stronger. Family first.

27

It's important to own and build a business.

Self sufficiency and providing for the future are key. Giving the generation that comes behind you a head-start is your responsibility. Being an employee only, will not usually lead you to wealth. Being an employee is not likely to give you the freedom and flexibility to do what you want to do or to focus on your family. With all these things in mind you must build a business that helps you by providing the needed financial income, resources and flexibility. Even if you start small or part-time, it is important that you start and begin to build. If you want to ensure that your kids have employment, then do what you can to build a business to employ them. You, leading by example, will have an amazing impact on your kids, those who participate and even those who watch your journey. If you care about the future, build businesses. In addition to building, ensure you proactively spend your dollars with those who value you and your community.

28

Learn about credit & debt.

If you want to maximize your efforts then utilizing credit can take you a long way. Unfortunately, at an early age many of us do not understand the importance of credit , how it works, and how it will impact our lives. Thus we are often taken advantage of or make critical mistakes. Once you have credit problems it's not easy to repair them.

Having good credit isn't a cure for all things and one can make it successfully through life without it. However having good credit strategically used right can definitely minimize many challenges and can be a significant asset.

You should build credit early, protect it, and leverage it. You should learn ways to maximize credit and because credit impacts personal and business ambitions. Strategically utilizing credit can help build wealth and achieve dreams.

29

Learn the value of money and how to use it for your benefit.

I'm sure you have heard "Money is the root of all evil" and perhaps it gives you a jaded perspective about money. Being objective I would definitively say, "Money is not the root of all evil." In fact, in the world we live money is necessary if you want to do good or do wrong. There is little execution or impact without financial resources. Unfortunately, many people with money only use it to get more money and for selfish means.

You must create money and use it to positively impact your life and that of others. It's not all about giving it away; money can provide you with "freedom" to do what you want to do. To spend time with your family, to volunteer, to explore, to research, to give your kids opportunity you never had. It's important to value money early in life, but it's more important to master it and never let it control you or change your character. Money is a great tool, make it and use it as such.

30

Buy land early in life.

They aren't making any more of it on planet earth. Get some, and get it as early as you possibly can. Have a strategic plan, budget, and put money away to buy. Make this a priority. Land can be used to help build wealth in many ways. Land can be used to provide a place for your family for generations to come. Land can be used as leverage to build business. You will always be faced with challenges of things you want and where to spend your money, do not squander or waste on things that will depreciate or have no value.

When thinking about what to do with your savings, be sure acquisition of land and property are at the top of your list. If purchased smart it will increase in value and be an asset to your life.

31

Do not waste your time, money or your words.

When you are young many things with the exception of money seem to be abundant, so with them we are often wasteful. Sometimes we experience peaks when money seems to be in abundance so we aren't as careful about how we spend it. We must learn to be intentional about everything; we must not waste. Time is short and resources are limited. Not everyone is worthy of the time you spend with them or the words you speak to them. Everything comes at an opportunity cost, so do your best to invest and choose wisely. You won't always know the first time what sorts of things and people are a waste, but once you learn, live what you have learned.

32

In our world, time and money are usually the only 2 things that substitute for each other.

If you haven't noticed we live in a world in which most people trade time for money. Another key thing to recognize is life is measured in time (years). So many people are in fact trading their life for money. Having money allows you to 'buy' another person's time, to do or perform a service for you. Having enough money also allows you to 'buy' your own time, allowing you the ability to own your time and your life, effectively not having to report to someone else that you have to sell your time to.

So be careful of what you do with your time, and how you spend and make your money. Protect your time and invest it wisely, because no matter what ; you can't get any more of it.

33

Time is more valuable than money.

Time(the minutes in your life) cannot be replenished, reissued or bought; when you are at the end of life, it is indeed the end of life. Time is the most important thing to life. What you do with time can give you many things, (money, experiences,toys and assets), but time stands alone in its value. Use it wisely, intentionally and with purpose. You won't get any more of it, and you don't know how much more is promised to you from this very moment.

34

Money is not everything, but life will be hard
to deal with properly without it.

Nope, money isn't everything, but it is best to have it as opposed to not having it. Without money the simplest things become complicated, the smallest issues can cause great stress. Never let money rule over your life , instead use it as a tool to enrich your life and to positively impact the world and your future. Focus on creating passive revenue streams. It's important to gain financial freedom and the ability to "write your own ticket." Even having the purest heart, not being given to greed and a commitment to do good for the world; you will still need money to help make that happen.

35

To some people money means everything,
and you mean nothing in comparison.

The things we value show up in the things we do. Examining the world on a deeper level, you notice that even though we say humanity and people are important, the truth is: the world doesn't value people in general. This shows itself on many levels including our social and educational systems. People are used largely to gain profit and to run the corporate machines and systems. For instance, there are many issues we could solve in this world that would help us greatly, but doing so wouldn't be profitable, so we continue to let the problems go on. Your interpersonal relationships are not safe from this lack of value for people, nor are you. Most are trying to "succeed" and most are taught that success is directly linked to money. Unfortunately many are so focused on this success that they will use, take advantage of and sell out others simply to get closer to their goals. Be aware of this when dealing with people, but most importantly, never be that person that doesn't value other people.

36

You hold the power to impact people and change the world.

Your actions, your way of thinking and the things you have learned shall all have an impact on your life. The intersection of your life with the lives of others has the power to influence them, and such influence compounded is world changing. Your purpose and vision can directly affect much and many. It can be the catalyst that sparks ideas and things for years and generations to come.

Never minimize your impact or your purpose. The world may be depending on it, even if they aren't presently aware of it.

37

Your legacy came from greatness and did not begin with slavery.

Slavery simply was not the beginning. We were kings and queens, we built great empires, we built the pyramids and other awesomeness that the world is still trying to understand. The whole world remains in awe of Egypt and other things across the continent of Africa. As an African people ruling over the continent we were creators and builders. Slavery interrupted our greatness, it was not the beginning of our culture or our people. It is said that a man should get knowledge, in all of your getting, get knowledge on your real history. Get knowledge about the continent of Africa. Get knowledge on the impact of africans throughout the entire world. Gaining such knowledge will prevent you from being a mental slave.

38

The "system" was designed to destroy you if ever given the chance.

We are judged by a different set of rules. As a black man in America we do not receive the same treatment. The system that we are told is there for us, the system that is to protect us, and keep us from injustice, is actually strategically against us. Any mistakes we make the system will be used against us to help bring our down-fall and destruction. We have to work exceptionally harder and overcome greater obstacles to receive the same accolades yet if we make any mistakes we tend to be judged harsher and more frequently than others. Knowing this early gives you the opportunity to be strategic in the execution of your goals and in the navigation of life. No degree of "success" will totally exclude you from this. Even if you personally seem to have risen above it, be careful not to forget that your situation is unique and millions of others are still subjected to the 'war' against them. You must not forget about them or leave them behind.

39

You will make mistakes, but it won't be the end of the world, push through and carry on.

Don't be afraid to do things, to try things. If you have an idea or a vision, go for it! You can't win or succeed at anything if you do not attempt that thing. Even when you think you have a perfect plan, there will be mistakes; learn from them, grow from them and keeping moving. Writing your own story will come with learning, mistakes and growth. The results of your story has the potential to impact many.

40

There are few things in life without reason.

Everything will NOT make sense. You will not be so special that you will understand all things you encounter. Sometimes you will be without the needed information and insight to make things makes sense. Sometimes people simply do things that have absolutely no logic or reason to them. There will be things and occurrences that are beyond the control and reason of men and mankind, and will leave you wondering "Why?". It is okay to question them, but do not get stuck on them. Sometimes you will get better understanding and insight later, but maybe you won't. Either way, keep moving forward.

41

Be loyal but don't hold on to those that mean you no good.

Be loyal to everyone that you have in your circle. You shouldn't expect loyalty if you yourself do not give it. Understand that not everyone holds these same principles. When you realize that people aren't loyal and that they don't mean you any good, it is critical that you make the decision to put them at a distance. Do not let your emotions hold you in a place that could allow them to harm your life forever.

Loyalty is an essential elements to ALL relationships, both business and personal. Make it part of your core characteristics and lead by example.

42

Nothing is forever, and most people, things and situations are merely temporary. Know when it's time to move on and do so without remorse, hesitation or animosity.

There are few people or things that will be in your life forever. Things and people will come and go. Some that may seem like they will be around forever will often end up leaving at some point or another. You yourself will be one of those that won't be around in someone's life that is expecting you to be there forever. All relationships and positions in life do not last forever. When it's time to move on... GO! Do not let any emotion keep you tied to that moment that has expired. The moment no matter how sweet must not keep you from the future.

43

You are temporary to other people.

JB

You are no exception, be it your choice or theirs, there are very few people that you will be a permanent "fixture" in their life. Just as people will walk out of your life for their reasons, you will walk out of the lives of others for yours. Not all relationships last forever. This is not always a negative thing. Ensure you make the best of all relationships in the moment, value them, give to them and learn from them. Do not seek to end them without reason, but do not be naive in thinking that every relationship will last a lifetime. Be honest enough to admit that you will be the 'cause' of the ending of many of them.

44

Just because people tell you they love you doesn't mean they wont hurt you

No one is excluded from causing others pain, even those who say they love you. In your life you must be prepared for emotional pain at some point or another. Here are a few things to keep in mind:

- Just because one hurts you doesn't mean that they don't love you.
- Some people will tell you they love you as a way of getting close to you in order to hurt you.
- Don't miss out on or deny yourself love just because you have been hurt by others in the past.
- All pain caused to you by others isn't intentional and meant to hurt you.
- The truth can be painful and needed.

Pain can destroy you or make you stronger, the choice is yours.

45

Your health is important, treat it as such…
ALWAYS.

As far as any of us know, we only get 1 life and we do not get do overs. Most material things in life that seem important have only temporary value or they can be acquired again. This is not the case when it comes to your health and body, thus you must take care of your health NOW. We all know someone or have heard about someone with a terminal illness or someone thats suffering from a ailment that negatively impacts their life every day. Your goal should be to take a preventive approach. This requires gaining knowledge about food, vitamins, herbs and staying active and in good physical shape. One of the most important elements is to ensure you are eating real food and not "food like product" that the industry is readily offering you. Learn how all things that you do or put into your body impact it and your health. Your good health will allow you to lead a long productive life without being a burden to those who love you.

46

Everything you read, and everything they teach isn't true. They have a reason for lying.

Seek many sources for things you are told, for the things you are told to read, and even for things that are presented to you as truth and fact. It's important that you find the opposing views to everything, research them, gather data from various perspectives, learn origins and about those who give you information, as well as what and who they are connected to. In America much of the history in the school text books are a lie and are carefully crafted to indoctrinate you and keep you away from knowledge and truth. We live in a world in which those who disseminate the information have a motive for shaping things in a certain way.

In a world where most people are told what to think and what to believe, one of your greatest assets is your ability to think for yourself; USE IT ALWAYS.

47

Learn the art of conflict resolution.

L ife will never be perfectly smooth, thats an unfortunate reality, we will have problems and disagreements with others. How you handle those problems and conflicts will have a significant impact on your life. As a man, you must be able to amicably resolve conflicts by merely using words. You should have the ability to stop things from escalating to full blown arguments or physical altercations, but to also turn the potential conflict into something of value. Relationships can be strengthened or destroyed when problems arise. When you master the art of conflict resolution you master the art of problem solving. He/she who masters the art of problem solving becomes invaluable. Be invaluable.

48

Learn to be a great communicator.

W ho doesn't love a great communicator? Communication is so very important to life, be it interpersonal , group or business marketing. Communication is a key element in getting what you want, in helping others, having others help you, resolving conflict and building teams. There is no effective or impactful leadership without great communication. Unfortunately we often mistake communication for talking to (or at)others, yet one of the biggest parts of communication is listening and understanding the other party. Learning to be a great communicator is learning to listen & objectively understand the position and perspective of others. One of the "problems" with communication, is most think they are better at it then they really are, thus we must continually evaluate it and work to improve it. If you are committed to success, use every opportunity to master the great art of communication.

49

Not everyone labeled a leader has the best interest of those they lead in mind.

Just because you are told someone is a leader; be they in education, politics, religious etc, it does not mean that such a person has the best interest in mind of those people that he/she is supposed to lead and care for. A critical element of leadership is serving those whom you represent and have been appointed by. One should constantly make decisions with these people in mind. Many leaders unfortunately are rarely without personal motive, thus it is important to know if their personal motives are in alignment with the needs/directives of the people they serve.

It is your life at stake, choose carefully who you follow, and be wise enough to know who isn't serving the interest of you and your people. Don't just merely listen to their words, watch their life, their actions, and their track record. This applies to you if you ever desire to lead as well.

50

Treat everyone right.

The world would be a much different and better place if we as individuals simply just intentionally treated everyone "right." The simple "Golden Rule" has the power to change the world if lived by : "Treat everyone the way you would like to be treated." There is currently much division; we are divided by ideas, religion, race, economics and anything else that can be pointed out as a difference. The world can supply enough for all of our needs, but not enough for our greed.

Each day and each situation, be consistent and intentional when making decisions that involve other people. Reflect and see things from the perspective of the roles being reversed and how you would want to be treated.

51

Seek a mentor.

Y ou can't learn everything on your own in your own lifetime, thus it is critical to find someone who has done it before you and soak their knowledge up like a sponge. Having a good mentor can not only give you knowledge beyond your years, but it can also open doors you didn't even know existed (as a result of their life and their existing relationships). Having a mentor doesn't mean they will dictate specifically what it is you do. A good mentor does offer you perspective and potential suggestions that you can use to think, evaluate and make decisions of your own. A good mentor will also be a bouncing board allowing you to get whats in your mind out and into the real world.

Find a someone who believes in you, who wants to see you win, that has experience in the area(s) you wish to dive, someone who has won, that will invest in making sure you win.

52

Not all elders are mentor material.

Sometimes people grow older and become wiser but sometimes young fools age to become old fools. Not all who are older are qualified to teach, advise or mentor those who are younger. It is important to select a mentor(and anyone who consistently pours into your life) very carefully and with intent and purpose. Based on your age and stage in life, your mentor doesn't have to be older than you(I've mentored a number of people older than myself). Keep in mind, not everyone has achieved significant and impactful results in life, so not everyone is "qualified" to help guide you on a path they know nothing about. Always be respectful to others, but only select a mentor that can add value to the process and to your journey.

53

Be a mentor.

JB

It's important to give back, and part of giving back is giving your time and knowledge to others to help them succeed in life. If you succeed at finding a mentor it definitely should be a commitment of yours to mentor others and aid in the positive impact of their life. Even if you do not feel that you are as successful as you wish to be, chances are your mere experience can be of value in guiding someone else down a path they have never embarked. *"In the land of the blind, the one eyed man is king."* No matter how green you are, you have something to give to someone younger and less experienced then you. Do not keep your experience and insight from them. Your influence, insight, perspectives and lessons could be the spark that sets someone on fire to do amazing things.

54

Someone is always watching you.

For good or bad your actions are always in the view of someone's eyes. Expect everything you do to be seen, recorded or tracked by someone. Some who are watching you will be inspired by your actions. Some who are watching will try to use what they see against you in a negative way. What you do each moment has the potential to directly or indirectly impact the future. It can positively motivate & influence those who watch your life or it can give someone a sense of hopelessness. It's not only what you tell people, but what you do and how you live when you think no one is watching. This has the potential to be your greatest or your weakest moment, and you may never know who saw it and how it will impact them. Remain aware.

55

Raw talent is a gift and curse.

Everyone is not born with raw talent, and on some levels raw talent allows you to stand out amongst those who do not have it. I can honestly say that throughout my life having 'raw talent' has been one of the things that has prevented me from reaching my full potential. Talent gives you the ability to crush your competition without putting forth your best efforts or without you focusing on becoming better. When you are younger, raw talent is the greatest separator between you and your competition; however as you get older and move up in the levels, everyone will have talent. There will also always be someone with more talent than you, but there doesn't have to be anyone who works harder than you or smarter than you. The separator at that point will be things such as discipline, strategy and on going learning(to name a few).

55

Raw talent is a gift and curse.

Moral of the story, do not rely only on your raw talent, it alone will handicap you and leave you unfit to compete on the highest level. Start with raw talent and use discipline to get better. If you depend only on your raw talent to win and you do not form other essential skills and disciplines that allow you to compete on the next level you will ultimately be defeated and unqualified to compete at the highest level.

56

Do not have kids with a woman unless you are committed to being with her for life.

There are many mistakes that one can potentially make in life, and many will argue which of them is the worst of all. Few would disagree that having kids with a woman you don't plan to be with is at the top of the list. In countless situations I have seem many lives disrupted, short stopped and simply torn apart by the drama that is often created when 2 people have a child with no specific intentions of doing life together and raising the child. Even in a "perfect situation" parenting and raising a child is no easy feat and is perhaps the greatest thing one might ever do in life. To be in a situation in which the parents aren't working together for each other or the best interest of the child is anything but ideal and should be avoided at all cost. Of-course not all situations go badly, but once a child is unintentionally conceived many of the details are out of your control. Control what you can, be intentional and be careful about when & who to reproduce with.

57

Your discipline or lack of it will shape your life.

There are few things more important than discipline. Once you have a vision or desire and you develop a plan, your discipline is the greatest determining factor in success or failure. Discipline, not talent has created more millionaires and more all star athletes. Lack of discipline has also left many behind, on just about every imaginable level. From everyday jobs to dreams of being the greatest in your field; hard work and discipline to do whats necessary is the only way it happens.

58

BE INTENTIONAL, about anything of importance

The things you want in life are in your control if you are intentional about achieving them. Thus you must be intentional with your time, your energy, your money and your other resources. Keep a specific end goal in mind, and make all of your moves intentionally in alignment with such goals. Do nothing that is with-out purpose or that is out of alignment. There are few things of greatness that happen without someone having specific intent to make them happen. A mental state of "intentionality" will be of great value to you and your life.

59

Your brother is not your enemy.

As black male in America seeing and experiencing black males working together is no where near a common thing as we need it to be. This is a problem that begins early in life, we aren't taught to work together, to build together, to support each other and most importantly to respect and value the life of each other as it were own. Often times we are made to feel like we are in constant competition(over things that truly don't matter). We are often driven by ego into altercations and things that put us against each other vs having us work together. Sadly many young brothers are more upset by another brother stepping on their shoes than they are about a white police officer purposely and unjustly killing one of their peers. This has to stop, we must see the value in each other and intentionally work together to build bonds to support each other, as this is the only way we can build strong communities and families for a strong future.

60

Kids are of their parents.

JB

It is just about impossible to separate the influence from a parent to the life, habits, thinking and actions of a child. What kids see and are surrounded by have way more of an impact then simply what they are taught in schools. We often times put too much weight and value on the school systems and not enough on ourselves, the parents and the personal account-ability of the child. As adults, and as parents you have a responsibility to develop your kids at home. The core characteristics and respect will come from you, what you teach them and what they see you do. The habits, the way of thinking, the way they treat people are largely a result of the parents.

61

The system can destroy the world by destroying the minds of kids.

The world wouldn't be the world without the humans that live in it. It is our minds as individuals that lead to the shaping of everything else. Thus if you corrupt or destroy the minds of the youth, then the future of the world has been destroyed with it. It is unfortunate that we live in a world (and largely America) that seems to intentionally create dynamics that work against developing kids and youth into productive, thinking members of society that will have positive impact on the world. As a youth working your way through the public educational system one must be very careful to not get caught up in many of the traps. You must also be 'lucky' enough to have instructors that care and are equipped to help you navigate effectively. Without that, much dysfunction & destruction awaits. Such strategic systems create a large population of non-thinking sheep and allow the few to effectively take advantage of the masses . Good for them, but bad for the world.

62

The world doesn't care about black people.

The current conditions of my era prove that largely: "The world doesn't care about black people." In all actually, the facts lead to the reality that: they are systemically attempting to eradicate us and make it appear as all of our culture and creations are their own. As far back as I can find historical accounts this has been the case since we allowed others into our territories and space. This was definitely true in my fathers era(I wish he would have told me). From the days of slavery in the US to the era of peaceful MLK, and "by any means necessary" Malcolm X, little has really changed. In America and across the planet all one has to do is open their eyes and see the war that has been raging against Africans/Blacks everywhere. Of course the dynamics and the details change, but the end goal remains the same. Eliminate, eradicate, suppress and take over. Don't expect them to care for you, expect them to come for you. Be prepared on all levels starting with your mind and open eyes.

63

You are not a minority.

∪B

Minority means "less", being of smaller percentage. As I began to have open eyes to the entire world and not just America, this really made me curious as to why blacks, and others are considered minorities when the reality is: those whom deemed us to be minorities are actually in the minority. This is simply another lie I was told (and believed) that I wish my father would have told me.

You are not a minority, people of color make up the majority of humans on the planet earth. This 'lie', is simply a base part of mental training and psychological warfare designed to start you with a negative perception of self. Do not believe it, do not embrace it. You are the majority, be 'major'.

64

Life Changes Fast.

This moment is this moment. How things presently are, they aren't promised to be in the future. For good or bad, things can happen in an instant, these things can have immediate and "permanent" impact on your life. People die that you have just seen, you could loose a job, or have an unexpected and sudden illness. Life throws things at us that are out of our control that can have negative consequences. Take nothing or no one for granted. However just as negative things happen in an instant, so do opportunities and possibilities that can put you in a position you only dreamed of. Whatever your goals and your dreams, it is your responsibility to be prepared and ready to take advantage of any opportunity that will put you closer to such success. You must also be prepared to not loose your mental sanity and your grip on life in the event of an unexpected tragedy. It's not what happens, but how you handle what happens that determines your life.

65

You can't control everything.

Some things are simply out of your control, even your most well planned efforts will not go as you have expected. People, weather, technology, etc. will throw wrenches in your execution plans. You can plan for most things, but everything will not be under your control. To know this is to know that you shouldn't let such things bother you or impact you on an emotional level. Maintain emotional control and logical thinking to devise the best solution for a situation. Calmly and consistently doing this is a critical element at mastering control and doing well in life.

66

Most things in your life, you can control.

JB

Your discipline, your decisions, your actions, and your thinking give you great power over your life. I'm not saying it will be perfect, or that there won't be situations beyond your control, but what I am saying is : "If you intentionally get knowledge, apply discipline, make as wise decisions as you can, and follow that with action; you won't make excuses, you will make things happen." Be committed to not being an excuse maker. Be committed to not putting your future in the hands of someone else. Be committed to being ready. Be committed to taking control and delivering results. Taking control means powerful things shall be commanded by you.

67

The people you love won't always be around.

There will be people you love; family, friends etc. that you will come to expect to always be in your life. This unfortunately will not always be the case. In life people die, get married, move, have a change in priorities or even tragedies. Any of these things and more can lead to the disconnection of what once was a vital relationship for your life. It is important to not let this get you off track. Value the memories, the things learned and the time spent but focus and move forward.

68

Do what you can, with what you have, right where you are.

The time will rarely ever be perfect, so do not wait on the right time or the perfect dynamics. Make it a point in life to take action(no matter how small) from the very place you are right now. Small steps consistently taken will change your position, power, perspective and resources. All of which, can have an impact on what you can and will do. Present action is key to your future evolution. Small steps taken today(and consistently everyday) can build great things for the future. Begin now!

69

You don't have to do anything wrong for a person to dislike you; but you don't have to care either.

Not everyone will like you. Sometimes this is a result of something you have done to them(knowingly or unknowingly), or sometimes it is for absolutely nothing that you have control over. Do not ever let this bother you or get you stuck on trying to figure out why or how you can change it. Resolve misunderstandings whenever possible but know that, "How a person feels about you doesn't have the power to impact your life unless you are focused on how they feel about you". It is also important to take correction when 'needed'. Not 'caring' about how they feel about you, doesn't release you from your necessity to constantly self reflect, self evaluate and make correction in your life.

Focus on your mission, continue to grow self and be committed to do good.

70

Think deeply and often.

ᴊB

In world that provides constant messages, distractions, lies and few things are without motive; there is absolutely no substitute for thinking. You must think deep, think often and most importantly you must think for yourself. It is critical to keep all of your senses open and aware, using them to intake everything. It is with this information that you must think and process. You must be careful not to consume too much media and news, as it attempts to tell you what to think. It is important to look and study beyond the present situation, as few things are without back story and history; find and examine this history. In all things, situations and stories use logic, alignment and coherence. Do not overlook details and do not ignore the obvious because of emotion or loyalty. Do not let peer pressure or tradition 'limit' or shape the scope of your thinking. It is your ability to think that will shape your life and it's impact and influence on your family and the world.

71

Have fun and enjoy life.

JB

Some people believe that there is no balance between work, purpose and fun. You get to live only 1 time, take it seriously, but enjoy it deeply. Have fun and get new experiences. Spend time with people you like and love. Just because you have purpose doesn't mean you can't have fun. There is absolutely no point in life if you can not enjoy it.

72

Travel and explore the world.

Go! Do! See! There is much in the world that is worth seeing. There is much to explore, much knowledge to be gathered, and there are plenty of interesting people to meet and engage. Never miss an opportunity for a travel experience, but more importantly, be intentional about it; as it will change your life. The world is so much bigger than your neighborhood, city, state, country. Experiencing other cultures, seeing things from other peoples perspective can be extremely enlightening and eye opening. Having a global world view puts you in a position many will never get to understand.

73

Tomorrow may never come.

Waiting on tomorrow is a lousy way to go through life. If you can do it now, if you can begin it now, DO IT! Things change, challenges come, people even die(you included). There are limitless possibilities that have the power to prevent "tomorrow" from coming. Do not procrastinate, move as if it must be done today. Do not let your dreams, ambitions or goals get stuck waiting on tomorrow. In fact today is the only day that you have the power to impact tomorrow.

74

Make today count, you will never get it back.

Today is one of the most important(if not the most important) day of your life. The present moment is the only moment that you have direct control over your actions. When tomorrow comes(if it comes) you can not return to yesterday. Every 'today' is built directly on the back of each today that it follows. Today, be wise, take action and build for tomorrow. Impacting the future can only be done today. Do not procrastinate, do not wait on others and do not make excuses. Make today count.

75

Learn a different language.

JB

Englishisn't the only language and thinking that it is or that it is the "most important" can create a huge problem in your growth. If you want to travel and actually get to know and understand the people in the places you travel, knowing how to speak the language will give you a connection and understanding that's next to impossible otherwise. I've been in countless situations in which I could not speak the native language of those around me; I've been in the car with others who were communicating with one another and I had no clue of what they were saying. It's not a great feeling, it's a feeling of powerlessness and ignorance. You won't learn every language, so you won't always be able to avoid this, but do not limit your linguistics and communication to just English. Pick another language and learn it.

76

Start random conversations with people you don't know for no reason.

Meet people, learn from them. Be a sponge. Pour something into some-one. Make them smile. Master the art of being "nice" to people you do not know, and want nothing from(this also helps you improve on your communication skills). You never know what will come from the simplest of things, it may simply brighten their day(or yours), or it may turn to a life long relationship. There is much to learn in life and you have no clue of what you don't know and who you might learn it from.

77

You never know what someone else is going through or what's going on in their mind.

As humans we tend to look at things and people from our current perspectives. We view them from our current lens and we filter most things from that place. This is however a great problem, because it's limited and usually not very objective and fair. Often times we tend to forget how far we have come, and the positions and situations we were once in. As we encounter people in life we must keep in mind that we do not know what they are personally dealing with or going through at that moment. We have to remember, that it is not all about us. We have to think about the bad days we've had and how we rubbed someone the wrong way. As you encounter people give them the benefit of doubt, try to be helpful, encouraging and non combative. Make it a point to try and positively impact people when you encounter them despite their initial disposition. I'm sure there are times you wish others had done this for you. Be what you wish to see in the world.

78

Everyone needs help sometimes.

Without any exception known to me, no one is always at their absolute best. No one knows it all, and no matter the heights we have achieved there is always another level to get to. Some people are born into bad situations, some fall from glory, but the commonality is simple : "We all need help from others sometimes(YOU included)." Don't feel less than a man when you need it or have to ask for it. *"No man is an island."* Thus, do not be afraid and do not let your ego talk you out of seeking help to get through things or to get to the next level. Not everyone will help you, but don't hinder yourself by being to proud to seek assistance.

79

You will be disappointed if you expect help
from everyone you have helped.

When you help someone, do it because you can and because it's what you want to do. Do not help others out of selfish motive or with the expectation that it is a bind for them to help you when you need help. Humans easily forget the things others do for them, and often times once the help is no longer needed, they act as if they never even needed it. Long story short; know that not all or not even most of the people you have helped will come to your aid when you need it. Do not waste time, energy or emotion focusing on this. Take notes and do what you must to move forward.

80

Some times it is better to turn the other cheek.

There are times in life that you must simply let things slide. Though your "ego" or manhood makes it difficult to just walk away, the battle or the person is simply not worth it. You have the power to make your own decisions, but you don't always have the power to decide the consequences of your decisions. It's important to know, not everything is worth your time or energy. Everything must be thought through, because once things are in motion they can escalate quickly. They can become emotionally driven and land you in a position of great regret, financial despair, physical harm or even death.

If there is nothing to gain, it is usually not wise to exert the energy. Think, measure and calculate quickly...your life is on the line.

81

Do not turn the other cheek, punish them
for their actions.

ᵁB

Crush Them! Break their backs! Eliminate their existence and all that stand with them! They must be punished for their actions and to prevent them from trying you again. All things can not be overlooked, and as man you must take action against those who have violated you or your family. Carefully evaluate if this is the decision that should be made. Do not make an emotional decision, it must be rational and sound. While principles should be factored in, its important to evaluate your principles and ensure they are worthy of being at the base of such decision making. You live in a world in which you are taught to be domicile and forgiving of your oppressors and those that harm you and your community(unless they look like you). In fact, you should be more forgiving of your "brother" than you should be of the system and people that operate with the purpose of harming you. Keep your future in mind. Execute without jeopardizing it.

82

Learn a tangible skill and you will never be broke or have to depend on the system.

ᴊB

You don't have to be tied to the corporate beast if the vision you have for your life doesn't include it. If you have tangible skills that others directly find valuable, you can always make money. In fact, depending on that skill and your work ethic, your income potential is largely limitless. Those skills can include such things as software programming, accounting, welding or carpentry(to name a few). You can maximize these skills to earn revenue, and use that revenue to work for you. Your 'freedom' depends on it. You do not have to subject yourself to merely slaving the best years of your life while looking forward to an eventual retirement to finally live life in old age. Design the life you want to live early, using a tangible skillset to help finance it.

83

No matter how much your mother loves you, she is a woman and can not teach you how to think or be a man.

There is no replacement for the impact of a real man or father on a son's life. There are simply things that women do not know about being a man. Things that women do not understand and can not transfer to a son. One doesn't know what they don't know, so they can't usually learn it. Seek the advice of men and get the perspective of men. It's important to get male mentors to pour into your life. Men that you can confide in, that you can bounce things off and sharpen thyself. The dynamics of life must be learned and understood from that of a man. Your mother's love for you can not replace the dynamics and uniqueness of manhood.

84

If she's not helping you build, then she is essentially helping to destroy what you are building.

There is great importance to maintaining a circle of people who are in some way helping or supporting your vision & efforts. Of those people there are few more potentially impactful than your female companion. You two, together should have a great synergy. You should be working together for a common goal. She should add value in some way to your efforts and your being. There is absolutely no in between, if she is not helping you build then she is eroding what you are building or negatively impacting your growth. Your goal everyday should be growth, and the person closest to you should be assisting in that growth(as should you theirs). Find someone that you are on the same page about goals, vision and end results. Do not waste your time; go with someone who helps the journey or go the journey alone.

85

Always remember: "She someone's daughter, and one day you may have a daughter of your own."

It kind of goes back to "Treat people as you would want to be treated". As male in this world, there are certain elements that sometimes and in some ways try and influence us to treat women as objects or not with the level of respect that may be due to them. Do not be that guy, treat her with respect, and if you feel she doesn't deserve your respect, then you shouldn't be in her presence(separate yourself from her). There is absolutely no in between; you should respect all women that are in your presence and avoid any women that aren't "worthy" of your respect. Do your best to positively impact and pour something of value into our women and young girls. Sometimes this will be 'correction' that will help them or give them better insight and respect for themselves. Do not ever take advantage of a situation or sister simply because you can. Your integrity is directly tied to how you treat people even when no one else knows.

86

Intelligence and loyalty is more important than good sex and being attractive.

There are many beautiful women in the world, and for the most part all of them are capable of providing sex, thus... this should not be a critical element in how you select one. It is instead important to select a woman who not only values intelligence and loyalty but who exercises those things as a way of everyday life. Your primary purpose of dealing with a woman should be to build a future, and she must be capable of helping you build. Build your vision, build your business, build your empire and build your family. I'm not saying she can't be attractive as well, but make sure her attractiveness comes with intelligence, loyalty, dedication and a commitment to truth.

Your choice in women has potential to greatly impact your life, your choices, your way of thinking and your results.

87

You can not teach those who do not want to learn.

When a person does not want to learn(despite the reason) they will not learn whatever it is you are attempting to teach them. You are wasting your time, as their brains are not open to receive. Focus your energy and efforts on those who are seeking to learn. Plant a seed, and perhaps it will grow, but do not force knowledge on those who wish not to have it.

88

Some people are more committed to their beliefs than they are to even knowing truth.

JB

The truth is : "The truth simply doesn't matter to most people". We live in a world of competing politics, religions, and competing messages that are broadcast by those who have an agenda. This is a world in which most simply want their existing beliefs to be true with no concern for the validity of them. People who stand in this frame of mind will not seek truth, and will often reject it simply because it does not align with their beliefs. No amount of evidence or proof will "convince" them; they have already decided. It is okay to respect the "beliefs" of others, but do not be burdened by them, and while it is wise not be forceful, you must not be afraid to impart opposing truth to them when 'necessary'.

89

Some people will resent/hate you for introducing them to truth.

They say "the truth will set you free", however most do not desire to be free(nor do they know what it is). No matter how simple or how serious, not everyone wants to hear the truth, especially about themselves, their family, things they already believe or something that they already have an allegiance to. By introducing the truth to those people, they will make you an enemy for disrupting their illusion with truth, facts and proof. If you live a life of seeking truth, standing by truth, then you must prepare for a life of potential conflict with those who stand against truth.

90

You will be judged based on your appearance.

C all it unfair or unjust, but you will be judged by your appearance. What you wear, and if you look professional or not; people will judge you and make assumptions about you. You can have the most genius mind-state, but if your pants are hanging off your butt and you aren't well groomed, most will not give you the opportunity to speak and if they do, most will not listen to the words you speak.

On the flip side, you can use this to your advantage; by keeping your appearance up-to par it can open certain doors that will then allow you to use your core skills, and personality to further your objective. Be intentional about your appearance, as it will be a tool in your arsenal or it will be another thing used against you. It is not only until you are 100% self sufficient and in ultimate power that your appearance will have less of an impact on your ability to succeed.

91

You can't help everybody.

JB

No matter how much you want to help everyone who needs it, the reality of life for most people is that it is impossible. The bandwidth in terms of time or financial resources simply doesn't allow. Often times trying to help everyone leaves less of an impact, and drains you. You will even encounter people that essentially don't want your help, that have little to no desire to help themselves or to fight for themselves, so choose who you decide to help wisely. Make helping others a regular part of your existence, but don't let helping others hurt you too much or you will not be able to continue in your positive efforts and impact.

92

Mind your business.

Focus on you and the things you need & desire to get done. Life is full of distractions, do not let them invade and overtake you. Do not pull distractions and problems into your life by worrying about other people and their lives. It is easy to get off track and hard to get back on. Many opportunities are missed by being off track because of distractions. Be so focused on your goals, your plans and your execution that you do not have the time or energy to give to anyone else's "business".

If there are great things you wish to accomplish in life, then you must give great effort to them. Minding your own business will put you light years ahead of those who can't focus solely on their own life.

93

Never give up.

101

THINGS

JB

If you are alive there is little to NO reason to ever give up. Before you begin anything, make sure that what you are about to pursue is 'worth it' to you. If you determined that it is, then win or loose…finish what you start. This will develop you in ways I can't explain. Life will present you with many challenges and distractions, they will come as financial problems, relationship 'drama', death of love ones and more; you have to focus and keep moving despite these challenges. Keep focused on your end result. Consult your mentors for support and help, but do not loose hope and do not give up.

Some people want to WIN and some only wish to play the game; your commitment to never give up puts you in position to win against all odds.

94

Be willing to die for a cause.

We will ALL die. There is no exception for you or for me. There are many theories on why we even live and how we got here, but no one definitively knows the answer to this. I think that while you are here it is important to do something of such a great purpose that you are willing to die for it. Something that you would do without payment, something you are proud to leave behind as as part of you legacy. You may decide this intentionally or you may discover it on your journey.

95

Know how to fight to live.

JB

Although we will all die, you should do everything(within reason) to live as long as you possibly and productively can. Sometimes this will require you to fight, both literally and figuratively. You must know how to navigate all the elements and segments you have to deal with. This includes business, everyday obstacles,health, family and the conflicts that will arise. Be mentally and physically prepared to deal with the opposition that is attempting to crush you.

96

You can't succeed at what you don't try.

To win you have to compete. Do not be a spectator at life. Dive in, do things, compete and discover what you are good at. You won't like everything you try but decide what you like enough to master. You won't fail if you don't try, but you can't win if you do not try. Failing isn't the end of life, often times it is the beginning of learning. People will often criticize you for not winning all of the time, but those who do so are usually mere spectators and have never competed. Winning starts with beginning, so get started and continue to do things and you will eventually make a habit of winning.

97

You don't have to fit in.

In today's world there are groups and clicks for everything and everybody. It is both a combination of separation and inclusion. This begins at a young age on a social level (before we even realize what is taking place), and it continues into our adult life in the realms of workplace, politics and financial "hierarchy". As you navigate life you will be expected to fit into boxes society has created. Peer pressure will lean on you and you will be expected to conform to predetermined way(s) of thinking and actions of the groups that surround you. You do NOT have to conform, you do not have to fit in, and you do not have to think as they think. While I'm not saying : "Do not be a part of groups." and I'm certainly not saying: "Do not be a team player." I believe working together as a group and a team is an essential element to life and progress, but what I am saying is: "Be your unique self; think, create, dream and do as you wish without being a sheep or a blind follower."

98

Trouble is easy to get into, but hard to get out of.

JB

No one told me (at least that I can recall) that trouble was easy to find and fall into, but is usually hard to get out of. Thinking back to as early as elementary school, I was a "rebel" of sorts, and in one way or another I stayed into something. Though I rarely looked for trouble, I also didn't always do my best to avoid it. Sometimes trouble found me, and some of the trouble that has found me has managed to even cause me problems in life, 20 years later.

Having the opportunity to know in advance that even the tiny decisions you make will have great impact, can change your thinking and doing. Think everything through, question it's potential impact on your life, on the life of your family and the life of others. Is it worth it? What's the point? If there is no purpose, then avoid it. Your future will thank you for it.

99

Constant learning has a way of changing
what you think you know, and certainly what
you believe.

JB

I constantly remind myself : "He/she that knows all, will learn little to nothing." One of the most important aspects of life is learning-- constant and deep learning. With just a little more living and learning, I consistently found that things that I was convinced I knew, I did NOT know. As you move through life learning and experiencing more things you will have the opportunity to overlay what you have learned in different areas; this gives you a different perspective and view. It allows you to see truth, to see lies, and it definitely gives you new questions.

What you think you know today, may not be true tomorrow. Your present beliefs won't always be your future beliefs. Stay objective, stay open and it will leave you in a unique position .

100

To build a legacy and leave something behind.

Your moment in time is important, but it's not all about you. You have a responsibility to build for the future and those that shall come behind you. None who follow you, and especially none from your direct lineage should be starting from zero. They should be able to build on what you have started and left behind. There are few things (if any) more important than this thing. Leave behind a great reputation, with great relationships. Leave behind knowledge. Leave behind financial resources. Leave behind land and property. Leave behind direction and purpose. Leave behind a culture and a systematic approach for building the future beyond one's self.

Live your life now, but do not neglect building a future and a legacy.

101

Your family's future depends on what you do with your life.

This goes back to legacy. Your life is important, and not only for the time period in which you exist, but for the future of your family. Keep this in mind when making decisions. It is your responsibility to make a path and to build a platform for your family to start. Leave knowledge, truth, resources and relationships behind. If you don't set a path and leave some direction, chances are your family will start without a clue of what to do, how to do, and without the resources to begin doing it. Too many of us have been left in this position because no one thought to be proactive in creating the future for us. This is a vicious cycle(that you perhaps have felt the impact of), this is a cycle that you can and must break -- starting NOW.

My Pledge to My Son

To my son _____, I
promise to devote my life to providing a better
future for you. I am devoted to teaching you
everything I have learned. I will do all I can to
teach you about the mistakes I have made. I am
committed to your learning and to transfer of
knowledge and integrity into your life. I am here
to support you in all ways that are needed. I am
here to listen, to talk and for you to simply lean
on. I am committed to not only help provide
mentally for you, but to give you a financial foun-
dation upon which you can build upon. I am not
perfect, I have made many mistakes, but I will be
here for you in any way you need as your father
and as your friend. We will navigate and achieve
together and you will do the same with your chil-
dren.

_____
Name   Date

My Pledge To My Father

To my father _____, I promise to value you, your time, and your input. I will not take you for granted. I will remain committed to learn what you teach and to better myself and our family. I will make a positive impact on this world and I will never give up. You will always be proud of me , the things I do and simply to know I am your son. I shall continue the traditions we began and I shall extend the legacy we are building together.

_____   _____

Name   Date

About The Author

JASIRI BASEL

Jasiri Basel is a native of Baton Rouge, Louisiana. Mr. Basel's life

experiences have included that of a single parent house hold, however at no point did he let this shape his life or his results. Starting a path to serial entrepreneurship early in life he has achieved some great successes that have led to unique insights and experiences. He has had the opportunity to rub elbows and match wits with some of the world's greatest innovators and executors. His life has also given him the ability to travel the world, experiencing many places, countries and continents. Such travel and experiences has allowed him greater perspective and field of view on the world. Through it all, it has not been without it's share of challenges and problems. He has never forgotten where he came from, what those before him have gone through and he has learned about his ancestors and their greatness. All of these things stand at the core of his commitment to do all that he can to positively impact, influence and create pathways for those who come behind him on this journey. This book is written from his perspective, that of a black male going through life and determined to succeed and help others do the same.

Acknowledgments

In remembrance of my father Louis "Smokey" Jackson, I didn't know you well but from others have said, you were a great man.

Special thanks to a few of the men who helped shape my life:

Trenton McElroy
Adolph Ray
Charlie Banks
Francis Hardnett
Coach Joel Hawkins
Robert Bennett
Coach Sam Lopez
Leslie Parms Sr.

A shout out to my sister Calandra Brown Robinson and a very special thanks and appreciation to my mother Edith Brown, who sacrificed more than I probably know for me to have some of the opportunities that began me on this journey.

64558230R10123

Made in the USA
Charleston, SC
28 November 2016